This book is dedicated to all the hardworking individuals who have had to adapt to the new normal of working from home. Your resilience and adaptability in the face of change are truly inspiring. As you embark on your remote work journey, let this guide be a compassionate companion, lighting your path towards mastering the art of working from home.

"Work is not a place you go to; it's what you do." - Unknown

FOREWORD

The world has dramatically shifted in how we work in the past few years. The home has replaced the traditional office environment, and the commute has been reduced to a walk from the bedroom to the home office. This shift has brought challenges and opportunities, requiring us to adapt and learn new working methods.

Mastering the Art of Working from Home" is a timely guide that addresses these challenges head-on. It offers valuable guidance and tactics to assist you in navigating the world of remote work, whether it is about creating an efficient workspace, using technology and AI, or managing a healthy work-life balance.

As someone who has worked from home for several years, I can attest to the value of the insights and tips provided in this book. They have helped me stay focused and productive while caring for my physical and mental well-being.

Whether you are new to working from home or an experienced remote worker looking to improve your skills, this book is valuable. It is filled with actionable advice you can apply immediately to your daily routine.

I hope that "Mastering the Art of Working from Home" will help you make the most of your remote work experience and find joy and fulfillment in this new way of working.

Happy reading!

[Stephen E Idahosa]

PREFACE

The COVID-19 pandemic has forced many people to work from home, and this new normal has brought about unique challenges and opportunities. However, to make the most of this situation, you must know how to navigate it effectively and efficiently. That's where "Mastering the Art of Working from Home" comes in—it is a comprehensive guide that provides you with all the knowledge and tools you need to succeed in your home office.

This book is a treasure trove of practical tips, hacks, and strategies to help you create a comfortable, ergonomic workspace that suits your needs and preferences. You will learn to establish a healthy and flexible routine that balances your work and personal life while communicating effectively and collaborating seamlessly with your colleagues and clients.

Moreover, the book will teach you how to manage your time, energy, and attention to avoid burnout and distractions and leverage the best tools and practices to optimize your performance and creativity. You will also learn how to maintain your well-being by caring for yourself and your loved ones.

Based on the author's experience working remotely for over a decade and the latest research from industry experts, "Mastering the Art of Working from Home" also features real-life stories and examples of successful remote workers sharing their challenges and solutions.

Improve your home office skills and gain flexibility by reading this book. You will also learn how to turn your home into a place to grow, thrive, and achieve your goals.

Ready to get started? Let's dive in!

ACKNOWLEDGEMENT

I want to start by expressing my appreciation to all the remote workers worldwide. Your experiences, challenges, and successes have inspired this book. Your stories have enriched the content and made it more genuine and relatable.

I am grateful to my family and friends for their support while I was writing this book. Their patience and encouragement have been invaluable.

I would also like to thank my editor, whose keen eye and insightful feedback have greatly improved the quality of this book. Your dedication and professionalism are truly appreciated.

A special thanks to the research teams and experts in remote work. Your groundbreaking studies and innovative ideas have provided a solid foundation for this book.

Lastly, I would like to acknowledge the readers of this book. Thank you for your interest and trust in this guide. It will serve you well in mastering the art of working from home.

INTRODUCTION

[1]"Choose a job you love, and you will never have to work a day in your life." - Confucius.

* * *

Flexibility and better work-life balance[1]

Flexibility and better work-life balance[1]

As we open the pages of "Mastering the Art of Working from Home," this quote by Confucius resonates with the essence of this book. In the following chapters, we will explore how to transform our homes into spaces that facilitate work and inspire passion and creativity. This book is a testament to the belief that when we love what we do and where we do it, work ceases to be a chore and becomes a source of joy and fulfillment.

The Rise of Remote Work

The concept of remote work has evolved. It's remarkable how this approach has revolutionized work and life.

Allow me to provide you with a brief overview of its evolution, and you'll understand why it's a trend that's here to stay.

1. ***Pre-Industrial Revolution:*** Before the Industrial Revolution, most individuals worked from their homes or farms.
2. ***Industrial Revolution:*** The Industrial Revolution shifted work from small-scale to large factories and offices,

bringing workers together en masse. Has had far-reaching consequences for the economy and society.

3. ***Invention of the Internet:*** The creation of the Internet during the 1980s opened up remote work opportunities. It has since revolutionized the way we work. Companies and individuals can now operate from anywhere, anytime, benefiting from increased productivity, lower costs, and a better work-life balance.

4. ***Telecommuting***: Did you know that "telecommuting" was first coined by Jack Nilles, a NASA engineer? Interestingly, in 1973, IBM conducted a test with a small remote team. The team grew to 2,000 by 1983, which is a testament to the success of telecommuting as a working model.

5. ***Digital Age:*** The digital age ushered in a paradigm shift when Tim Berners-Lee published the first website on August 6, 1991. This event paved the way for the rise of garage startups and an era of technological innovation.

6. ***COVID-19 Pandemic: The*** COVID-19 pandemic in 2020 accelerated remote work adoption, with many companies implementing remote work policies to ensure employee safety.

The future of work is remote these days, with more and more companies opting to adopt remote work policies after the pandemic. It's worth noting that most work throughout history has been remote, with office cubicles being the exception.

Benefits of working from home

Many organizations have embraced remote work due to its benefits, including increased flexibility and a better work-life balance. It has also become necessary for businesses in light of recent events. Below are some of the benefits that come with adopting remote work.

1. ***Less time spent commuting:*** Working from home presents several benefits, including eliminating lengthy commutes and the ability to devote more time to personal hobbies and social activities. This flexible work style allows for a more favorable work-life balance, leading to a more gratifying existence. By prioritizing remote work, individuals can optimize their personal and professional lives.

2. ***Increased productivity and performance:*** A common observation among professionals is the increase in productivity when working from home, which is attributed to the absence of potential distractions that could hinder task completion.

3. ***Improved work = work-life balance:*** Remote jobs can allow you to tailor your workday to your preferences through flexible schedules.

4. ***Location Flexibility:*** Imagine working from anywhere with a strong, stable internet connection and no restrictions. You can achieve an excellent work-life balance and greater productivity from home, a cafe, or traveling.

5. ***Setting Your Hours:*** With remote work, you can take control of your work schedule and maximize your productivity by working during the hours that suit you best.

Challenges of working from home

While working from home offers several benefits, it is also vital to consider the potential challenges. Recognizing these challenges will help find the right balance and determine what works best for remote work.

1. ***Time Management Challenge:*** Some may need a

    traditional workday structure to maintain track of time. Errands can turn into window shopping, and short walks can become hours-long neighborhood tours.

2. ***Isolation:*** Social isolation is common in remote workplaces, leading to feelings of disconnection and loneliness among team members.

3. ***Distractions:*** When you work from home, it can be challenging to stay focused and maintain motivation, particularly if you share your space with family, spouses, and friends.

4. ***Overworking:*** Remote work can lead to needing help to draw a clear line between work and personal time. These blurred boundaries can lead to extended working hours, which means less time to relax and unwind —difficulty in controlling schedules and prioritizing personal times to achieve a healthier work-life balance.

5. ***Communication Challenge:*** Due to the rise of remote work, digital communication has become the new standard. However, remote work sometimes challenges communication, requiring more face-to-face interaction. It is essential to be aware of such challenges and take steps to overcome them for effective collaboration and productivity.

The challenges of remote work are manifold. Nevertheless, these hurdles can be managed and overcome by implementing effective strategies and appropriate tools. The key to success is identifying the most suitable strategy for one's unique remote work setup. By leveraging one's strengths, utilizing available resources, and experimenting with different approaches, optimal productivity and job satisfaction can be achieved while overcoming the challenges inherent in remote work.

SETTING UP YOUR HOME OFFICE

"Your work will occupy a significant portion of your life, and satisfaction can only be achieved by doing what you truly believe is great work. The key to doing great work is to love what you do." Steve Jobs.

* * *

As we delve into the chapter on setting up your home office, let this quote guide us. It reminds us that our workspace is more than just a physical location; it's where great work happens. It's a place that should inspire, motivate, and make us love what we do even more. When you work remotely, it's crucial to have a comfortable and productive home office tailored to your needs. To achieve this, you need to create an efficient workspace that is functional and enjoyable.

Home office set up.

Here are some practical tips to help you start and set up a work area to make your remote work experience more comfortable and productive.

Choosing the right location

Suppose you're fortunate enough to have a dedicated room. In that case, you're already one step ahead in creating the perfect space for your needs. However, there's no need to worry if you don't have that luxury. Many creative ways exist to maximize unused corners, large closets, or space underneath your stairs.

For instance, a corner of a room can transform into a cozy reading nook with a comfortable chair, a lamp, and a small side table. Adding a desk, chair, and storage shelves can quickly transform any small closet into an efficient home office space. Suppose you have a staircase in your home.

When choosing a spot for your workspace, it is essential to consider the availability of natural light and the proximity to power outlets.

The possibilities are endless for creating a functional and stylish space in your home. You can make the most of any corner or unused space with creativity.

Essential Office Equipment

A reliable computer and stable internet connection are essential for video conferencing and cloud-based tools.

Working on a smaller screen for long hours can lead to eye strain. An external monitor provides a larger screen and significantly reduces eye strain, enabling you to work longer and more comfortably.

You can upgrade your typing and navigation experience with the convenience of a wireless keyboard and mouse. Avoid using tangled cords or limited mobility with a wireless mouse and a full-size keyboard that can enable you to work comfortably and efficiently at your desk or even from the comfort of your couch.

A high-quality webcam is essential for productive video meetings. Using noise-canceling headphones lets you concentrate and focus better, particularly in noisy environments.

Desk and Chair: An ergonomic chair and a desk at the appropriate height can substantially improve your comfort and productivity. Comfortable furniture encourages good posture during prolonged working sessions. A docking station or USB hub can also be handy when connected to multiple devices.

Finally, having good lighting can significantly improve the quality of your video calls. Not only does it help to reduce eye strain, but it can also ensure that you look your best on camera. Consider investing in quality lighting to elevate your video conferencing experience.

Creating a productive environment

- **Privacy Matters**: Create a designated workspace with privacy dividers and curtains to maximize productivity and concentration. This will allow you to separate yourself from distractions and focus on your work.
- Your home is your canvas, waiting for you to unleash your creativity. With decor, you can opt for the understated or go wild—it's all up to you!
- **Think about shared space**. If the area is shared, plan accordingly. Set up partner desk setups to accommodate simultaneous work. If needed, provide seating and table space for clients.

- **Invest in quality furniture and supplies**. A comfortable chair, an ergonomic desk, and lighting are essential for a productive workspace. The furniture should have designs that organize your computer, keyboard, mouse, and other tools.

- **Decorate to boost mood and productivity**: Adding your favorite items, such as colors, plants, or artwork, can make your space more unique and personalized. Keeping it free of clutter is also essential, as this helps you maintain focus and stay on task.

- **Create a schedule**. Establishing your work hours and ensuring you adhere to them is essential. Additionally, taking breaks to stretch and rejuvenate yourself is crucial for your productivity and well-being.

- **Dress up for work**. Give yourself a little push to get into work mode. A straightforward way to do this is to change out of your pajamas and into some work clothes. This slight shift in your routine can help you get the right mindset to tackle your day.

- **Separate business and personal finances**: Do not mix your personal and business finances. Take action and separate them! By keeping your finances distinct, you can stay organized. Tracking your business expenses can help you better understand your business and personal expenses, making claiming tax deductions easier.

Due to personal circumstances, a software developer working in the marketing department of a biotech company had to switch to fully remote work shortly before the pandemic. As a single parent to a special needs child, they had to set up a home office that would allow them to balance their professional responsibilities with their parental duties. They found that having a dedicated workspace and a routine helped them manage their time and responsibilities effectively.

Remember that your home office can transform into a space that reflects your style, enhances productivity, and makes working a pleasant experience. Imagine how productive and efficient you could be with a well-designed home office. Picture yourself unlocking your full potential and achieving your goals more quickly and efficiently in the right environment. It's possible. You have the power to make it happen. Invest in yourself and create the space you need to thrive.

TIME MANAGEMENT

"Time is what we want most, but what we use worst." William Penn.

* * *

As we go through the chapter on time management, let's keep this quote in mind, emphasizing the significance of utilizing our time wisely, mainly when working from home. It highlights the necessity of employing effective time management techniques to improve productivity and maintain a healthy balance between work and personal life.

Time maps

Working from home can be an excellent opportunity to enjoy the comfort of your own space while still being productive. However, managing your time effectively can also be challenging, especially with the many distractions and competing priorities in a home environment.

Here are some intelligent time management tips to help you stay productive and maintain a healthy work-life balance:

Setting a routine:

Building your routines starts with creating your workday schedules, setting boundaries between your work and personal time, and incorporating flexibility to help you stay focused and avoid burnout while pretending you are going to the office to switch into work mode mentally. As part of remote work routines, scheduling and utilizing regular breaks can enhance productivity and prevent burnout. Take a break from your workstation, stretch, and recharge.

Balancing work and personal life

Balancing work and personal life is crucial for well-being and happiness in a remote work environment. However, it can be challenging. The following strategies may help:

- ***Establish boundaries***: a healthy work-life balance while working remotely is crucial. Setting boundaries between your personal and professional lives can help you achieve this balance.
- ***Keep Consistent Hours:*** points to consider are:

Work the same hours daily

Be consistent with your routine

Separate work time from personal time

- ***Disable or Limit Notifications:*** To protect your time and minimize distractions, turn off unnecessary notifications and customize the ones you need. Disable notifications from non-critical apps and adjust the frequency or type of important alerts to avoid constant interruptions.

- ***Use Technology Wisely:*** Utilize communication tools and productivity techniques to manage your workday efficiently and complete tasks on your to-do list.

- ***Make your health a priority.*** When working remotely, losing sight of your physical and mental health can be easy as the boundaries between work and personal life become blurred. To maintain your well-being, it is essential to take care of yourself consciously. This means taking breaks regularly to stretch your legs or have a snack, exercising to keep your body active and healthy, and eating a balanced diet to provide your body with the necessary nutrients. Additionally, it's essential to address any mental health concerns you may have, such as stress or anxiety, by practicing mindfulness techniques like deep breathing or meditation. Remember, prioritizing your health will make you feel better and improve your work performance.

It's important to remember that finding the right balance in a remote work setting is a personal journey, and what works best will depend on your specific circumstances.

Tools for scheduling and organization:

Staying productive and maintaining a structured work routine can be challenging when working from home. Fortunately, many effective scheduling and organizational tools can significantly enhance your productivity and help you stay on track. Some of the most valuable tools include:

Scheduling Tools:

- ***10to8:*** An online platform for scheduling appointments across any channel, including over the phone and online, can assist you in automating tasks related to staff organization.

- ***Loom***: Loom is an application that enables you to record and share your screen and webcam for training, presentations, and sales outreach. Visual demonstrations are an efficient way to communicate and explain concepts or processes.

- ***Microsoft Office 365:*** Microsoft's suite of tools provides a range of features to streamline your workflow. With Outlook, you can easily manage your emails, calendar, and appointments in one place. **OneDrive** offers secure cloud storage for all your files, accessible from anywhere. With Word, you can easily create and edit documents using various formatting options and collaboration tools.
- ***Google Online Suite:*** Google offers productivity tools like Google Calendar, Google Drive, and Google Docs. Google Calendar helps schedule meetings; Google Drive provides cloud-based storage and file sharing; and Google Docs is a powerful document creation tool with real-time collaboration. These tools allow individuals and businesses to work more efficiently and effectively.

Organization Tools:

- ***Slack:*** Slack is a cloud-based communication platform for modern teams. With Slack, you can organize conversations into channels, share files, connect with external apps, and integrate with existing tools. You can also create and assign tasks, set reminders, and keep track of progress all in one place. Slack is user-friendly and intuitive, making it easy for teams to communicate and collaborate effectively, whether working remotely, in the office, or on the go.
- ***ProofHub*** is an all-in-one project management tool designed to help businesses of all sizes. It offers a comprehensive set of features that include planning, collaboration, organization, and project delivery. The tool allows you to create project plans, assign tasks to team members, set deadlines, and track progress. You can also use ProofHub to collaborate with team members in real time, share files, and communicate via chat. The tool has a simple and intuitive interface that makes it easy for anyone to use.

- ***GanttPRO:*** GanttPRO is the ultimate online project management tool. It empowers you to schedule tasks, collaborate with your team, and track progress efficiently using state-of-the-art Gantt charts.
- ***Monday.com:*** Monday.com is a powerful work operating system with many features to help teams streamline their work and achieve optimal efficiency. With this platform, teams can quickly customize workflows to suit their needs, track project progress in real-time, and manage all their projects from a single, centralized location.

Regarding time management, finding what works best for you is crucial. It's a personal process that depends on your specific needs and circumstances. Adapt as you go.

To work from home, you need tools that suit your specific requirements. Use task management systems like **Trello, Asana**, or **Monday.com** for asynchronous collaboration. To monitor progress, use project tracking software like **Jira**, **Basecamp**, or **Microsoft Project**. When selecting a tool, consider ease of use, compatibility, and security. Choose the right tools to create an efficient work-from-home setup that helps you achieve your objectives while maintaining a healthy work-life balance. And happy remote working!

PRODUCTIVITY

"Productivity is never an accident. It is always the result of a commitment to excellence, intelligent planning, and focused effort." - Paul J. Meyer.

* * *

As we delve into the chapter on productivity, let this quote inspire us. It emphasizes that productivity, especially in a work-from-home setting, requires dedication, intelligent strategies, and concentrated effort.

Productivity

Work-from-home productivity has been a popular subject of discussion and research lately. According to studies, remote workers are more productive than those working in a traditional office. A study conducted by Stanford University found that employees who work remotely are 13% more effective than their counterparts who work in an office. However, remote work also has its own set of challenges that can affect productivity. Below, we will delve into some of these factors.

Overcoming distractions

Overcoming distractions while working from home is essential for maintaining productivity. Here are some practical strategies to help you stay focused:

1. **Set Clear Priorities:** At the start of each day, you must identify your priorities and create a to-do list with specific time slots allocated to each task to avoid getting sidetracked with irrelevant work.

2. **Time Blocking:** To increase work-from-home productivity and focus, you should divide your day into blocks of time, each dedicated to specific tasks or groups of related tasks. This approach lets you prioritize your work and focus on one task at a time, boosting productivity and better time management. This strategy is also known as time blocking.

- Dedicate the first hour of your workday to checking and responding to emails. Spend the next two hours completing a specific project. Use the hours after lunch to attend to other things or conference calls.

- For successful time blocking, be realistic with time estimates and adhere to a schedule. You can manage your time more efficiently and accomplish more daily with practice.

3. Family Matters: Balancing work and family can be difficult. To make it easier, it's essential to communicate with your loved ones about your work hours and set routines for your kids during your peak productivity times. If you need extra help, consider calling in grandparents or other family members. Hanging a "do not disturb" sign is an excellent way to minimize disruptions and distractions when you need privacy or quiet time. This sign will let others know you don't want to be disturbed or interrupted.

4. Avoid digital temptations: The internet is a vast space with unlimited information and entertainment at our fingertips. Still, it is crucial to use it wisely and establish healthy habits to manage our time. One way to do this is by setting aside time for specific online activities and turning off notifications for non-essential apps and websites, like checking emails, browsing social media, or playing video games. Additionally, using browser extensions to block specific websites or apps can help us focus on important daily tasks. By setting clear boundaries and developing healthy habits for internet usage, we can make the most of our online time without letting it overpower our lives.

5. Household Chores: It's important to avoid multitasking during work hours and to set aside specific times for chores like laundry, cooking, and cleaning. Additionally, using a visual calendar can help manage your tasks.

6. Blurred Work-Life Lines: Remote work blurs boundaries. Establish a dedicated office space to separate work and personal life mentally. Use noise-canceling headphones to block out distractions. It's essential to be aware of your schedule and take regular breaks.

Remember, while distractions are inevitable, adapting, finding, and implementing effective strategies can assist you in staying focused and achieving your goals—productivity in your work-from-home setup.

According to the Harvard Review study, employees often must be available to their colleagues and managers around the clock. Availability is not limited to working hours alone. A team of researchers at Microsoft revealed that during the pandemic transition, even those employees who had previously established firm boundaries between work and personal life found them blurring. Despite these findings, other research indicates that managers are still concerned about employees' productivity when working from home compared to working in the office.

Setting goals and tracking progress

Working from home can be challenging, demanding self-discipline and effective goal management.

To ensure productivity and success, it is essential to establish a routine and set clear objectives.

Several strategies can be used to set goals and track progress. Here are some strategies to set goals and track your progress:

1. **Define clear objectives**: Establish specific and measurable work-from-home goals that you want to achieve. Keeping track of your progress and maintaining focus on your goals is crucial. Utilize project management tools such as **Asana** to provide detailed instructions, set deadlines, and communicate expectations effectively with your team.

2. **SMART Goals:** To achieve your goals effectively, ensure they are SMART. This acronym is specific, measurable, achievable, relevant, and time-bound. These guidelines will help you create clear, quantifiable, attainable goals pertinent to your life and bound by a specific time frame.

- Break down larger objectives into smaller, manageable tasks. Please make sure to set a deadline for each task.

3. **Goal-Tracking Apps:** Leverage goal-tracking apps to stay organized and focused. Consider using apps like **ClickUp**, which consolidates goal-related data, progress tracking, and more on one platform. Subscriptions can be tailored to meet the specific needs, preferences, and requirements of businesses and teams of any size.

- Other options include **Strides Coach. Me** and My **Way of Life**. These applications assist you in establishing, monitoring, and illustrating advancement toward your objectives.

4. Visualize Progress: Use charts, graphs, or visual trackers to monitor your progress. Seeing your achievements visually can motivate you.

- Tools such as **ATracke**r enable you to monitor your time on particular objectives.

5. Regular Check-Ins: Review your progress regularly. Adjust goals if needed.

- Maintaining clear communication with your team or supervisor ensures everyone is on the same page and addresses any challenges.

In achieving your work-from-home project goals, it's essential to maintain consistency and be adaptable. Remember that these two factors play a crucial role in ensuring success.

Tips for staying motivated

Staying motivated while working from home can be challenging.

However, implementing effective strategies such as setting specific goals, taking breaks, and creating a designated workspace can help you maintain focus and productivity.

1. Create a Schedule: When working from home, it's essential to have a structured workday. Set clear start and end times for work and stick to your schedule as closely as possible. It helps you focus on your goals and effectively complete your tasks. Please ensure that time stays put.

2. Establish a Dedicated Workspace: Creating a designated work area helps your brain focus and develop a productive mindset.

It is essential to separate your workspace from your leisure areas. Although it may be tempting to work from your bed, doing so can negatively impact your sleep.

Therefore, it's best to reserve your bed for rest and intimacy. Instead, consider setting up your workspace in a different location, such as the kitchen or living room.

It can help you feel more organized and productive while creating a clear separation between work and relaxation.

3. **Set Daily and Weekly Goals:** Planning your work goals daily can significantly improve your productivity and help you stay on track.

To start, dedicate a few minutes each day to reviewing the tasks and assessing their priority level. Once you understand what needs to be done, consider breaking down big tasks into smaller, more manageable ones. Helping you focus on one specific aspect at a time can also help prevent feeling overwhelmed. Maintaining focus and motivation is crucial when working towards your goals. It's important to pace yourself and take on only a little at a time to prevent you from getting overwhelmed with tasks. And be realistic with your time. Taking on too much can cause burnout and reduce your productivity in the long run. With consistent practice, you'll be able to manage your workload and achieve your desired outcomes effectively.

4. **Make Time for Breaks:** Short breaks between tasks are essential to maintaining productivity and focus throughout the day.

These breaks will help you refresh your mind and body, allowing you to return to work with renewed energy and concentration. Taking at least five minutes to step away from your desk during these breaks is recommended.

Take a quick walk, do some stretching exercises, or sit and relax. By incorporating these short breaks into your daily routine, you'll be able to work more efficiently and avoid burnout.

5. **Use Time Management Techniques:** If you wish to manage

your time effectively, use time management techniques. One of the most effective methods is to log your time for each task.

It helps you identify tasks that take up most of your time and lets you plan your schedule accordingly. You can also use software and apps that track your time on different tasks and provide detailed reports.

These techniques can improve productivity, reduce stress, and improve work-life balance.

6. Take Breaks Outside: It's essential to take regular breaks from work to help you stay productive and focused. When taking a break, try to spend some time outdoors and enjoy the natural environment.

Being in nature can help you feel refreshed, reduce stress, and boost your creativity, whether it's a quick walk in the park or a mountain hike. So, take a few minutes to step outside, breathe in the fresh air, and let the beauty of nature inspire you.

When working from home, it's essential to establish a structured routine and maintain discipline to stay motivated and productive. It means setting aside specific hours for work, taking regular breaks, and avoiding distractions such as social media or household chores during work hours. Creating a comfortable, organized, and distraction-free workspace can be helpful. Maintaining a well-structured routine and following these valuable tips, you can maintain productivity and motivation while working from home.

COMMUNICATION

"The single biggest problem in communication is the illusion that it has taken place." George Bernard Shaw.

* * *

As we explore the chapter on communication, let this quote remind us of the importance of clear and effective communication, especially in a remote work setting. It emphasizes the need to ensure that our messages are sent and understood.

Communication

In today's world, communication has become an indispensable part of our daily lives, especially in remote work situations. We use different methods of communication to establish connections with colleagues, clients, and friends across the globe. With the help of modern technology, we can communicate effectively and efficiently from the comfort of our homes or workplaces. Virtual meetings, online classes, and webinars are a few examples of how we can communicate remotely.

These platforms not only help us exchange information but also assist in building relationships and fostering team collaboration. Using technology, we can bridge distances and bring people together, regardless of their physical location. Technology has revolutionized communication, making remote work more comfortable and productive. Communication has become vital in our lives, particularly in remote work scenarios.

Practical online communication tools:

Online communication tools facilitate interaction, information sharing, and collaboration among people regardless of location. They're crucial in modern workplaces. Common types include:

- **Instant Messaging (IM)** Instant messaging platforms are the perfect solution for individuals or groups who require quick and efficient communication. With platforms like Slack, Microsoft Teams, and Whats App, you can stay connected in real-time through text-based messages.
- **Video Conferencing:** Video conferencing tools like Zoom, Google Meet, and Microsoft Teams are powerful communication platforms that allow people to connect and collaborate remotely. These tools have various features that facilitate face-to-face interaction, including high-quality

video and audio capabilities, screen sharing, and real-time messaging. They enable virtual meetings, presentations, and discussions, allowing people to collaborate seamlessly regardless of location. In addition, the tools can cater to users' needs, ensuring ease of use and accessibility. In doing so, they could increase the efficiency and productivity of remote communication.

- **Email:** Email as a means of communication is crucial. Especially when working from home. It offers numerous benefits, such as convenience, cost-effectiveness, and Eco-friendliness. Unlike traditional mail, email doesn't require postage or paper, making it an environmentally friendly option. Moreover, email lets us send messages and documents instantly, eliminating the need for physical delivery.

- **File Sharing:** File-sharing services such as Dropbox, Google Drive, and One Drive. have become essential for remote work and digital collaboration. They provide a secure online space to store, access, and share files with individuals or teams across different locations, devices, and platforms. Collaborating with others is easier with real-time notifications, change tracking, and comment features. Along with their primary features, these tools can connect with other productivity tools, enhancing their overall functionality." email clients, project management software, and communication platforms.

- **Collaboration Platforms:** Use team collaboration and project management tools such as Monday.com, Asana, or Trello to improve team productivity. These tools enable effective team communication, file sharing, and project management. For instance, Monday.com will allow you to create custom workflows, track time, and visualize project timelines with Gantt charts. Asana allows you to assign tasks, track real-time progress, and manage projects efficiently. Trello uses the Kanban method to design boards and cards for organizing tasks and projects.

- **Intranet:** An intranet refers to a restricted network only accessible by authorized individuals or employees of a particular organization. It provides a centralized platform to share information, including announcements and resources, among employees.

It is essential to remember that the selection of communication tools should be based on your team's specific requirements and preferences. This applies whether you manage a remote team, collaborate in an office, or work remotely alone. It is crucial to choose the right tools. as they can substantially boost productivity and teamwork.

Etiquette for virtual meetings

Virtual meetings have become a standard part of our daily routine in today's remote work environment. Although convenient, upholding professionalism and effective communication during these meetings is crucial. To achieve this, here are some best practices that one should follow:

Arrive on time (and end on time):

- It is essential to schedule a specific time and inform all participants well to ensure a successful meeting.
- A recommendation is to encourage team members to join a few minutes early to avoid delays.
- Schedule a follow-up or email a post-meeting summary if the meeting goes overtime.

Avoid Multitasking:

- Stay engaged during the meeting by focusing solely on the discussion.
- Turn off notifications and avoid checking emails or other

apps.

- Treat the presenters and other participants with respect.

Notify Others Before Leaving:

- If you need to leave a meeting early, inform others beforehand.
- Sudden departures can disrupt the flow and cause unnecessary delays.

Test your equipment in advance:

- Ensure your camera, microphone, and internet connection are working correctly.
- Make sure you suitably position your camera and choose an appropriate background for your video.

Dress Professionally:

- Even in virtual meetings, dress appropriately.
- Please ensure you adhere to any specific dress code guidelines the company provides.

Introduce yourself before speaking.

- Especially during audio-only calls, introduce yourself before contributing.
- Identifying the speaker when communicating with others is essential to clarify and avoid confusion.

Mute Yourself When Not Speaking:

- To avoid disturbing background noise during your video conference or call, mute your microphone when you're not speaking. This will help keep the audio clear and prevent unwanted distractions for other participants.
- Please unmute yourself only when you have something to contribute.

Use video whenever possible.

- Video enhances connection and engagement.
- Please turn on your camera unless there is a specific reason

not to do so.

Be mindful of your environment.

- Choose a quiet, well-lit space for your meeting.
- Please make sure to eliminate any potential distractions and create a professional background.

Virtual meetings are essential for remote work, and good etiquette ensures effective collaboration and respectful communication.

According to a study conducted by Microsoft, more than 61,000 of its employees experienced becoming more isolated in their communication and engaged in fewer real-time conversations while working from home. The study also revealed that remote workers spend fewer hours in meetings, which could make acquiring and sharing new information more difficult. This may have implications for productivity and innovation in a full-time remote workforce.

Staying connected with your team:

Remote workers must maintain strong connections with their teams. Here are some effective strategies to foster collaboration and camaraderie:

- **Daily Conversation**: Make time for casual chats with colleagues. Interactions, whether quick messages or virtual coffee breaks, help build relationships and combat isolation.
- **Regular Team Check-Ins:** Schedule frequent team meetings or check-ins. Video conferences allow face-to-face communication, which is essential for maintaining team bonds. Platforms such as Zoom, Google Meet, and Microsoft Teams make collaborating easier for groups.
- **Recognize Employee Efforts:** Acknowledge and appreciate

your colleagues' contributions. Regular recognition boosts morale and reinforces a sense of belonging.

- **Mentoring Programs:** Pair remote employees with mentors within the organization to foster professional growth and provide a support network.
- **Live Working Sessions:** Collaborate virtually to brainstorm, problem-solve, or co-create. Schedule joint work sessions.
- **Stability Through Rituals:** Establish consistent routines like weekly team updates or virtual coffee meetings. Predictable patterns create stability and a sense of continuity.
- **Set Clear Boundaries:** Remote workers should be encouraged to maintain work-life balance by defining clear boundaries. They should know when to disconnect and recharge.

Remote teams need to make intentional efforts to connect and engage. Implementing these practices allows remote workers to stay connected, motivated, and aligned with their teams.

HEALTH AND WELLNESS

"Health is a state of the body. Wellness is a state of being." J. Stanford.

* * *

As we venture into this chapter, let's remember the significance of maintaining our physical, mental, and emotional well-being as we delve into health and wellness, mainly when working from home.

Wellness

Maintaining health and wellness while working from home involves addressing physical and psychological aspects. Here are some tips to help you achieve that:

Prioritize nutritious eating for a healthy diet. Your meals should include fruits, vegetables, whole grains, and low-fat dairy products in balanced portions. Choose healthier alternatives to foods high in sugar, salt, and unhealthy fats, as they can harm your health. Making the right choices for your body will make a difference quickly.

Stay hydrated by drinking enough fluids regularly. Please keep it simple by sipping water or other beverages that you enjoy. Remember to drink more fluids when it's hot or you're exercising.

Regular exercise is essential for both the body and the mind. It offers numerous benefits, from physical health to mental well-being.

Setting up a comfortable home office is essential to prevent physical strain. Maintain optimal posture and comfort to avoid any physical discomfort.

Maintain a work-life balance by keeping your work separate from your personal life.

Practicing mindfulness can be an effective technique to reduce stress.

Personal connections through social interaction help alleviate isolation.

Pay attention to your body. Symptoms like headaches, a sore back or neck, and dry or tired eyes may indicate excessive screen time.

Everyone's needs are unique, so finding what works best for you is essential. Please take care of yourself!

The Importance of Taking Breaks

Don't let the comfort of your home office fool you. It's crucial to take regular breaks while working remotely. Stretch your legs, clear your mind, and come back even stronger. Remember, taking breaks isn't a luxury; it's necessary to maintain productivity and focus. Even if they are short, you can take a few minutes to stand up and stretch, take a quick walk, or step away from your workspace for a little while. It's essential to take breaks because of the following:

1. You can solve problems better when you periodically take a break and do something different.
2. Taking regular breaks can lower the chances of mental burnout.
3. Taking breaks and moving around is essential to prevent physical issues resulting from prolonged sitting.
4. Breaks can improve your mood and overall well-being.

Breaks can improve your work, so take some time off throughout the day. After a break, you are more likely to be focused and productive. Maintaining optimal physical and mental health requires certain essential habits, and taking regular breaks is undoubtedly one of them.

To deal with physical activities, I found an interesting blog post titled '19 Remote Workers Reveal Their Biggest Challenges. You can find the link to the post here:

https://clockify.me/blog/remote-work/challenges-remote-work/.

Earl White, a real estate attorney, worked in an office for years until he started working remotely in March 2017. He noted that the sedentary lifestyle that comes with working from home has led to various health-related problems. Despite his job not involving physical labor, he used to move around regularly by commuting to work, attending meetings, or taking a walk to a nearby store. However, being stationary while working from home caused him to gain weight and experience back pain, making it difficult to be productive.

To tackle the issue, Earl decided to change his work routine. He purchased a standing desk, a yoga mat, and a chair with lumbar support to help him maintain a healthy working posture. Additionally, he now walks before work and after lunch to stay active and reduce the adverse effects of his sedentary lifestyle.

Exercises for remote workers

Various challenges as a remote worker include incorporating exercise into your daily routine. However, there are numerous exercises that you can perform. Right at home, that will help you stay healthy and active. Here are three exercises that you can achieve with confidence:

1. **Planking:** Strengthen your core muscles with exercise. Move your chair to one side and clear the floor around you. Lie facing the floor and prop yourself up with your forearms and toes. Keep your head, torso, and legs straight, forming a downward-sloping line. Hold this position for as long as you can.

2. **Leg lifts while sitting:** To perform this exercise, maintain a straight back and flatten your feet on the floor. Lift your legs off the ground, straighten them, and rest them on an imaginary stool. Hold the position for 10 seconds, then gradually lower your feet. Repeat this exercise about 12 times.

3. **Stationary Curls:** This exercise strengthens your biceps and improves your posture. Look for a small weight on your desk, such as a closed water bottle or a heavy stapler. Hold the object in front of you with your arm outstretched, parallel to your thigh, and your palm facing the ceiling. Grip the object and bend your elbow to curl the weight towards your chest. Pause for a

moment, then slowly lower the object back down.

Adding these easy exercises to your daily routine can make a big difference. Keep at it and stay confident in your ability to remain healthy and active while working from home!

Mental health considerations

Although remote work has its advantages, it is essential to note that the practice can introduce adverse mental challenges to the well-being of employees. Hence, explore other methods and strategies that promote a healthy work environment.

Here are some key points to keep in mind:

Psychological Benefits: Remote work can have a positive impact on mental health, especially for individuals who experience anxiety.

Challenges of Isolation: Remote workers often feel lonely and anxious due to the isolation of working remotely.

Supporting Mental Health: Employers can support the mental health of their remote employees in various ways, such as offering mental health benefits, staying connected with technology, socializing virtually, checking in regularly, encouraging physical fitness, being flexible, rewarding good work, and promoting work-life balance.

Protecting Your Energy: It's essential to save your energy, support your team, and enjoy the mental health benefits of remote work.

Remember, it's crucial to be aware of these considerations and take steps to maintain mental health while working remotely.

BUILDING YOUR CAREER REMOTELY

"Success usually comes to those too busy to be looking for it." - Henry David Thoreau.

* * *

As we explore the chapter on building your career remotely, let this quote inspire us. It reminds us that success often comes to those working towards goals, even from home.

Online presence

Building a successful career in a remote work environment can be a fulfilling experience, but it demands a well-thought-out strategy and consistent efforts. One of the first things to consider is to assess your skills, interests, and career goals to identify the roles and industries that align with your career aspirations.

Networking Online

Join professional online communities, such as **Slack** groups and virtual communities, to connect with others in your field. Social media platforms are one way to use technology and reach a broad audience. Follow industry leaders, join relevant groups, and participate in discussions. Attend virtual events like webinars, online conferences, and virtual meetups related to your field to meet and connect with other professionals.

Consider utilizing remote-only job boards such as **FlexJobs**, **JustRemote**, or Working Nomads in your job search. Don't hesitate to contact people you'd like to connect with by sending a personalized message.

After meeting someone new, follow up with them to build lasting professional relationships. Networking is about making relationships over time, so be patient, persistent, and genuine.

Upskilling and online learning

It's essential to upskill and re-skill for career growth, especially in remote work.

Here are some strategies to achieve this:

1. **Online Video Courses and Tutorials:** Online learning platforms allow you to choose topics relevant to your job and interests and learn at your own pace.
2. **Certification Courses:** Completing a certification course online or through a community college can enhance your skills and make you more marketable.
3. **Podcasts** and reading books are great resources for acquiring more skills and a deeper understanding of a

topic.

4. **Volunteering:** Volunteering provides hands-on experience and helps you acquire new skills.
5. **A mentor** can offer valuable guidance, share knowledge and experiences, and help navigate career paths.
6. **Gamified Learning Techniques:** Gamification can make learning more engaging and fun.

Remember, continuous learning and innovation are essential to meeting the demands of the future of work. Remote workers can gain a competitive edge in today's and tomorrow's job markets by up-skilling and re-skilling. Best of luck with your learning journey!

Maintaining executive presence

Executive presence is a term that refers to a person's leadership skills, professionalism, and overall conduct in the business world. It encompasses many traits, including communication, time management, emotional intelligence, and continual learning. While working from home can be challenging to maintain an executive presence, it is possible with the following tips:

- -Maintain regular communication: Regular check-ins and updates with your team are essential to staying on top of your work and maintaining productivity. This ensures that team members know your contributions and progress towards your goals.

- - Professional environment: Since you are working from home, creating and maintaining a professional environment is vital. This includes having a dedicated workspace free from distractions and dressing appropriately for video calls to reflect a professional demeanor.

- - Time management: Good time management is crucial to maintaining an executive presence. It involves managing your time effectively and respecting your colleagues' schedules to ensure timely completion of tasks.

- - Active participation: Participate in meetings

and discussions to provide valuable input and shape project direction. Doing so shows your team members that their involvement is crucial in achieving the goals and objectives.

- - Emotional intelligence is a crucial leadership quality that involves being aware of one's emotions and those of team members. It also consists of demonstrating empathy and understanding, which can help promote a positive work culture.

- - Continual learning: In today's fast-paced and dynamic business environment, staying up-to-date with trends and developments is crucial for success. Continual learning enhances your knowledge and skills and helps you bring new and innovative ideas to the table. As an executive working from home, it is essential to maintain a strong and credible presence in the industry, which can be achieved by staying informed and continually seeking out new knowledge and experiences.

Remember, maintaining an executive presence is about how you present yourself and how you interact with others and handle your responsibilities. By following these tips, you can enhance your executive presence while working from home and continue to be an effective leader in the business world.

Navigating remote job opportunities

The COVID-19 pandemic has profoundly impacted how we work and live, leading to a significant shift towards remote work. This trend has resulted in many people seeking remote job opportunities that allow them to work from anywhere, offering numerous benefits such as flexibility, autonomy, and cost savings.

However, remote work has challenges like isolation, communication, and productivity. If you want to find and succeed in a remote job that aligns with your skills, goals, and lifestyle, here are some tips to help you navigate the remote job market.

1. Identify your strengths and preferences: Remote work is not for everyone and requires specific skills and traits to thrive. To increase your chances of success, you need to consider your self-motivation, time management, communication, collaboration, and problem-solving skills. It would help if you also considered your personal preferences, such as your preferred work environment, schedule, and level of interaction with others. Knowing your strengths and preferences will help narrow your search and target the right opportunities.

2. Resume and portfolio updates: Your resume and portfolio are essential tools to help you land a remote job. To make the most of them, you must ensure they showcase your relevant skills and experience for remote work. Highlight any previous remote work experience or projects demonstrating your ability to work independently, communicate effectively, and deliver results. Use keywords and phrases that relate to remote work, such as "remote," "virtual," "online," "telecommute," or "work from home." Include links to your online portfolio, website, or social media profiles showcasing your work.

3. Search for remote jobs on various platforms: Many companies, such as **FlexJobs** and Remote, specialize in remote job listings.co, **We Work Remotely**, or **Remote OK.** You can also use general job boards like **Indeed**, **LinkedIn**, or **Glassdoor** and filter by location or keywords to find remote jobs. You can join online communities and networks catering to remote workers, such as **Slack groups**, **Facebook groups**, or **Reddit forums**. These communities can help you discover new opportunities, learn from other's experiences, and connect with potential employers or collaborators.

4. Prepare for remote interviews: Once you land an interview for a remote job, you must be prepared

to impress the interviewer and showcase your fit for the role. Remote interviews are usually conducted via phone or video call. Hence, you must ensure a reliable internet connection, a quiet and professional setting, and a suitable device and software. You also need to practice your communication skills and body language, as they can make a big difference in how you come across on screen. Research the company and the role beforehand, and prepare some questions for the interviewer.

5. Negotiate your terms and expectations: If you receive an offer for a remote job, congratulations! You are one step closer to working remotely. However, before accepting the offer, you must negotiate your terms and expectations with the employer. This includes discussing your salary, benefits, hours, equipment, tools, communication methods, feedback mechanisms, performance metrics, and career development opportunities. You need to ensure that you are comfortable with the arrangement and that it aligns with your goals and values.

I found an interesting blog post titled "Networking Success Stories" on VocationVillage.com. You can see the link to the post here: https://www.vocationvillage.com/networking-success-stories/.

Highlights of the blog emphasized that:

Networking provides an effective way to connect with others professionally and beneficially. Building strong relationships with people can be very beneficial, positively impacting your career.

Communicate your message clearly and concisely to leave a lasting impression and create new opportunities.

Remember, "It's not what you know; it's who you know." By cultivating meaningful relationships, you can tap into a network of support and resources to help you achieve your goals and reach new heights of success.

 You don't have to spend countless evenings networking over cocktails to build a strong network. It can be as simple as staying in touch with former colleagues and nurturing meaningful connections.

Companies that face challenges with remote work:

As remote work became increasingly popular lately, especially during the COVID-19 pandemic. However, some companies have found it to be an unsuccessful model. As a result, some organizations that once allowed remote work have reversed their policies, requiring employees to return to the office, believing in-person collaboration and communication are necessary for success.

For instance, in 2013, Marissa Mayer, the CEO of Yahoo, famously ended the company's work-from-home policy, stating that increased collaboration and communication were necessary for the company's success. Best Buy followed suit around the same time, ending its flexible work program and opting for a more traditional office setup.

Similarly, in January 2023, Starbucks' CEO Howard Schultz demanded that all corporate employees return to the office for at least three days a week after struggling to implement a one-day return policy. General Motors also announced a return to work plan for salaried workers, starting from January 30. This was a significant change from the company's former policy, allowing employees to work remotely until a certain point.

Disney CEO Bob Iger recently announced that employees working from home must return to the office at least four days a week. This decision aligns with other companies like Apple and Goldman Sachs, which have also curtailed remote work, emphasizing the importance of in-person collaboration.

In a creative business like Disney's, connecting, observing, and creating with peers is irreplaceable when physically together. Bob Iger emphasized the value of learning from leaders and mentors in person.

While some companies have accepted an expanded role for remote work in hybrid arrangements, Disney's move signals a shift away from full-time remote work. The rise of remote work during the pandemic tripled the number of workers primarily working from home between 2019 and 2021, but companies are now seeking a balance between in-person and remote work.

So, the era of widespread work-from-home policies is evolving, and companies are navigating the best approach for their unique cultures and productivity needs.

These examples emphasize the challenges of remote work and the importance of finding the right balance for each company and its employees. While remote work offers many benefits, it may only suit some organizations.

In conclusion, remote work is a fulfilling and rewarding career option. Following these detailed tips, you can discover and succeed in a remote job that suits your needs and preferences.

LIFELONG LEARNING, TECHNOLOGY, AND AI

- "The real problem is not whether machines think, but whether men do." B. F. Skinner.

One of the most exciting developments transforming learning processes is **Artificial Intelligence (AI)**. AI has the potential to revolutionize remote education and work through personalized and adaptive experiences, enhancing learner engagement and providing opportunities for immersive and interactive learning and communication.

This chapter will inspire us to embrace lifelong learning fueled by the synergy of technology and AI.

Use of Technology and AI

Technology and AI are increasingly crucial in enabling remote working systems, especially after the COVID pandemic.

Technology and AI can help remote workers in various ways, such as:

- Providing real-time support: Technology and AI can offer services like chat bots and cybersecurity to assist customers and employees with common queries and issues without human intervention. AI-based chat bots like MongoDB's Drift Bot and Amtrak's customer service bot, Julie, can immediately assist incoming customers.

- Automating back-end tasks: Technology and AI can also take over some mundane and repetitive tasks that remote workers have to perform, such as marking attendance, maintaining records, generating reports, and scheduling meetings. This can save time, reduce errors, and improve productivity for remote workers. Google Calendar's Smart Scheduling feature utilizes AI to find the best time and place for a meeting based on participant availability and preferences.

- Enhancing video conferencing: Technology and AI can also improve the quality and efficiency of video conferencing, which is one of the remote workers' primary modes of communication. Technology and AI can adjust factors like lighting, background, and framing to make remote workers look more professional and presentable on camera. Technology and AI can also reduce file sizes, improve connections, and provide an intuitive user experience. Zoom has integrated AI into its products to achieve these benefits.

- Improving assessments: Technology and AI can also help remote workers with evaluations, such as performance reviews, feedback, and learning. Technology and AI can use data and algorithms to measure, evaluate, and certify the skills and competencies of remote workers. Technology and AI can also provide remote workers with personalized and adaptive learning opportunities to enhance their knowledge and abilities. LinkedIn Learning suggests courses and content using AI based on user profiles, interests, and goals.

- These are ways that technology and AI can help unite remote teams and improve operational efficiencies. Technology and AI can analyze data to help remote workers succeed.

THE NEED FOR DIGITAL LITERACY AND TECHNOLOGICAL SKILLS IN REMOTE WORK

Digital literacy and technological skills are crucial for remote work, enabling workers to effectively communicate, collaborate, and access information using digital tools and platforms. Remote workers must be proficient in various technologies, such as video conferencing, cloud computing, project management software, and instant messaging applications. They also need to adapt to new technologies and learn new skills as required by their work tasks and environment.

Some of the benefits of digital literacy and technological skills for remote work are:

1. Increased productivity and efficiency: Digital literacy and technological skills can help remote workers automate, streamline, and optimize their work processes, resulting in faster and more accurate work completion.

2. Improved communication and collaboration: Digital literacy and technological skills can help remote workers communicate effectively with their colleagues, managers, and clients, using various digital channels and modes to share information, feedback, and ideas.

3. Enhanced creativity and innovation: Digital literacy and technological skills can help remote workers generate and implement creative and innovative solutions by accessing and utilizing various digital resources such as online courses, podcasts, blogs, and forums.

4. Reduced isolation and stress: Digital literacy and technological skills can help remote workers reduce their isolation and anxiety by connecting and socializing with their peers and communities and accessing digital support and wellness services such as online counseling, coaching, and mentoring.

Therefore, digital literacy and technological skills are essential for remote work, enabling remote workers to perform their jobs effectively, efficiently, and enjoyably.

TECHNOLOGY VERSUS HUMAN SKILLS

Technology versus human skills is a topic that has been debated for a long time, especially in the context of the future of work. Technology has been progressing rapidly, with artificial intelligence (AI), automation, and robotics taking over many tasks that humans traditionally performed. However, it is essential to recognize that specific human skills, such as creativity, critical thinking, teamwork, and empathy, remain necessary and valuable in the workplace and society. In this write-up, I will explore the advantages and disadvantages of technology and human skills and how they complement each other.

Technology has many benefits for individuals, organizations, and the world. Technology can increase productivity, efficiency, accuracy, and innovation. Technology can also reduce costs, errors, risks, and environmental impacts. Technology can enable new possibilities, such as exploring space, curing diseases, and enhancing education. Technology can improve the quality of life by providing entertainment, convenience, and access to information.

However, technology also has some drawbacks and limitations. Technology can create ethical, social, and legal dilemmas like privacy, security, and bias. Technology can also cause unemployment, inequality, and displacement, as some workers may lose their jobs or skills to machines. Technology can also have adverse effects on health, well-being, and relationships, such as addiction, isolation, and stress. Technology can also be unpredictable, unreliable, and vulnerable, as it may malfunction, break down, or be hacked.

On the other hand, human skills are the abilities that make us uniquely human and differentiate us from machines. Human skills enable us to interact with others and the environment, think critically and creatively, solve problems and make decisions, and express ourselves and empathize with others. Human skills also allow us to learn, adapt, and grow, to cope with change and uncertainty, and to pursue our passions and purposes.

Human skills have many advantages for individuals, organizations, and the world. Human skills can foster collaboration, communication, and diversity. Human skills can also drive innovation, entrepreneurship, and leadership. Human skills can also enhance well-being, happiness, and fulfillment. Human skills can also contribute to social good, such as justice, equality, and sustainability.

However, human skills also have some challenges and limitations. Human skills can be difficult to measure, evaluate, and certify, as they are often subjective, contextual, and dynamic. Human skills can also be hard to acquire, develop, and maintain, requiring time, effort, and practice. Emotions, biases, and stereotypes can also influence human skills, affecting judgment, performance, and behavior. Human skills can also be scarce, unevenly distributed, and underutilized, as some may need more time to pay attention to them.

Therefore, technology and human skills are not mutually exclusive but complementary and interdependent. Technology can enhance human skills by providing tools, data, and feedback. Human skills can guide and regulate technology by setting goals, values, and standards. Technology and human skills can work together to achieve better outcomes, such as efficiency and quality, creativity and innovation, well-being, and social good. Technology and human skills can also balance and compensate for each other by filling the gaps, correcting errors, and overcoming challenges.

LIFELONG LEARNING AND UPSKILLING IN THE FUTURE OF WORK

Lifelong learning and upskilling are essential in determining the future of work. Advancements in technology, demographics, and social trends will impact the future of work. These factors will have varying effects on different industries. Workers must acquire new skills and competencies to meet the evolving needs of employers, customers, and society.

Some of the skills and competencies that will be in high demand in the future of work include

- **Upskilling**: Upskilling refers to acquiring new or additional skills to enhance one's existing skill set. It involves learning new technologies, tools, or techniques relevant to one's profession or industry. Upskilling is essential for individuals to remain competitive in the job market and enhance their employability.
- **Digital skills**: The use and development of digital technologies, including AI, big data, cloud computing, and IoT, will revolutionize sectors such as manufacturing, agriculture, healthcare, and education.
- **Future of work**: The future refers to the anticipated changes in work and employment due to technological advancements, automation, and other factors. It is characterized by the increasing use of artificial intelligence, robotics, and digital technologies in various industries.

Role of lifelong learning and upskilling: Lifelong learning and upskilling are essential in the future of work for several reasons:

- **Adaptability**: The future of work is expected to be dynamic and constantly evolving. Lifelong learning and upskilling enable individuals to adapt to new technologies, job roles, and work environments. It helps them stay relevant and employable in a rapidly changing job market.

- **Continuous improvement**: Lifelong learning and upskilling promote a constant improvement mindset. Continuously updating knowledge and skills enhances efficiency and effectiveness in the workplace.

- **Resilience**: Lifelong learning and upskilling build resilience in individuals. They enable individuals to navigate economic disruptions, job displacements, and industry transformations. By acquiring new skills, individuals can explore new career opportunities and mitigate the risks associated with job obsolescence.

- **Competitive advantage**: Lifelong learning and upskilling give individuals a competitive edge in the job market. Employers highly appreciate and value employees who take the initiative to develop their professional skills and knowledge. Such proactive employees are seen as assets to the company as they bring new ideas, perspectives, and creative problem-solving skills. In addition, possessing a diverse skill set is equally important as it gives the employee the ability to take on various tasks effectively. Employers are known to offer promotions, bonuses, and other benefits to employees who demonstrate a solid commitment to professional development and are skilled in multiple areas.

- **Future-proofing**: Lifelong learning and upskilling future-proof individuals' careers. Continuous learning and skill acquisition can help individuals keep up with technological advancements and automation. They can position themselves for emerging job roles and industries, reducing the risk of job displacement.

Lifelong learning and upskilling are crucial for the future of work. They enable individuals to continuously adapt, improve their skills, build resilience, and gain a competitive career edge. This is crucial for remaining competitive in the job market and improving employability, productivity, and well-being.

Upskilling and learning can help employees adjust to changing demands in various industries, allowing them to reach their personal and professional objectives. Furthermore, these skills contribute to their communities' social and economic development. They can help workers prepare for career transitions, promotions, or entrepreneurship opportunities.

In conclusion, technology and human skills are not in competition but can complement each other. Both are essential and valuable sources of competitive and comparative advantage. They can work together and learn from each other. As technology and human skills evolve, they can improve and adapt. Therefore, the future of work and society depends not on choosing between technology and human skills but on combining and integrating them.

ENSURING THE ETHICAL AND LEGAL USE OF AI.

"In the realm of AI, where innovation meets creation,

Let's tread with caution, with ethics as our foundation.

For in every line of code, in every algorithm's dance,

Lies the need for legality, fairness, and balance." Unknown

* * *

As AI becomes more prevalent in work-from-home situations, it has raised ethical concerns that individuals and businesses should consider.

AI realities

HERE ARE THE CRITICAL MORAL ISSUES THAT NEED TO BE ADDRESSED:

1. **Job Displacement**: Using automation and AI in specific industries may lead to job displacement, which could increase unemployment rates.

2. **Privacy and Surveillance:** AI-generated content raises concerns about privacy and surveillance, as it could inadvertently spread false information or incite violence.

3. **Bias and discrimination** can result from AI systems inheriting biases from their training data, leading to unfair outcomes. It is crucial to guarantee transparency and impartiality when it comes to decision-making that involves Artificial Intelligence.

4. **Intellectual Property Violations:** Generative AI may infringe on intellectual property rights or misuse copyrighted data.

5. **Data Privacy Issues:** AI systems that handle personally identifiable information (PII) can violate data privacy regulations

such as GDPR or CCPA.

6. **Inaccurate Usage of Generative AI Output**: It is essential to use the output generated by AI tools responsibly and accurately.

7. **Role of Human Judgment:** The philosophical challenge lies in determining the appropriate role of human judgment alongside AI decision-making.

To ensure that the use of AI remains ethical, businesses must navigate these complexities, stay legally compliant, and align their practices with societal values.

STEPS REMOTE WORKERS CAN TAKE TO ENSURE THEIR USE OF AI IS ETHICAL AND LEGAL:

1. **Understand AI Ethics:** Define what ethics means operationally.

2. **Tailor Your Message:** Tailor your message to your audience.

3. **Tie Your Efforts to Your Company Purpose:** Ensure your efforts align with your company's purpose.

4. **Lean on Trusted and Influential Individuals:** Seek guidance from trusted and influential individuals.

5. **Never Stop Educating:** Continuously educate yourself about AI ethics.

6. **Identify Existing Infrastructure:** Identify existing infrastructure that a data and AI ethics program can leverage.

7. **Create a Data and AI Ethical Risk Framework:** Create a data and AI ethical risk framework tailored to your industry.

8. **Change How You Think About Ethics:** Take cues from the successes in healthcare or other industries to change your thoughts about ethics.

9. **Monitor Impacts and Engage Stakeholders:** Regularly monitor the impacts of AI applications and engage with stakeholders to address any concerns.

Ethical AI involves implementing structures and processes to identify and mitigate potential threats rather than applying moral principles to corporate actions.

SOME ESSENTIAL REGULATIONS AND GUIDELINES THAT WE SHOULD KNOW ON THE USE OF AI:

1. American Bar Association's Resolution 604: This initiative is part of the growing efforts to regulate AI nationally and internationally.

2. European Union's AI Act: This act bans or limits specific high-risk applications of AI.

3. UNESCO's Recommendation on the Ethics of Artificial Intelligence: This is the first-ever global AI ethics standard adopted by all 193 Member States.

4. US Federal AI Governance: The White House, Congress, and various federal agencies have put forth a series of AI-related initiatives, laws, and policies.

5. AI Ethics in Companies: Codes of ethics in companies and government-led regulatory frameworks are two main ways AI ethics can be implemented.

6. AI Governance in Other Countries: Countries like the UK, Canada, Singapore, and China have their strategies and regulations for AI ethics.

These regulations and guidelines ensure that AI systems are lawful, ethical, and robust, respect data privacy, avoid bias, and do not cause unintentional harm. It's important to note that these regulations continually evolve as AI technology advances.

CONCLUSION

"The future depends on what you do today." - Mahatma Gandhi.

* * *

As we conclude "Mastering the Art of Working from Home," let this quote remind us that our actions today shape our tomorrow. It underscores the importance of making the most of our work-from-home experience today to build a successful and fulfilling future.

Remote work future

Working from home has become increasingly popular thanks to technological advancements, environmental concerns, and changing work preferences. However, working in an office requires a different mindset and skill set. To succeed as a remote worker, one must learn and apply the art of working from home, which involves several key factors.

Firstly, creating a comfortable and productive workspace is crucial. This can involve finding a quiet and isolated area, setting up a proper desk and ergonomic chair, and ensuring good lighting and ventilation. A conducive workspace helps you stay motivated and focused and avoid distractions and interruptions.

Secondly, setting a regular schedule and boundaries is essential. This can involve establishing a fixed workday and break times, communicating your availability to colleagues and clients, and avoiding the temptation to work beyond your designated hours. Maintaining routines and boundaries can help prevent burnout, maintain a healthy work-life balance, and maximize productivity.

Thirdly, communicating effectively with colleagues and clients is critical. It can involve various communication tools and platforms like email, chat, video conferencing, and project management software. You can do great by establishing clear expectations, goals, and deadlines and being responsive and proactive in your communication.

The Future of Remote Work

The future of remote work has become a topic of much discussion and interest, particularly after the COVID-19 pandemic made many workers switch to working from home.

According to some sources, the future of remote work will likely be a hybrid model, where some workers can work remotely for part of the week while others will return to the office or other physical locations. However, this scenario may vary depending on the workers' industry, occupation, and geography, as some jobs are more suited for remote work than others. Remote work presents advantages such as flexibility, convenience, and autonomy but also comes with challenges, including communication, collaboration, and work-life balance.

While remote work is not new, it has become increasingly popular in recent years due to technological advancements, environmental concerns, and shifting preferences. Studies predict that by 2025, around 32.6 million Americans will work remotely, representing about 22% of the workforce. This projection implies a gradual shift towards remote work arrangements, and as long as Millennials make up the largest workforce, remote work is here to stay.

Therefore, companies should be ready to adapt beyond 2024. The future of global remote work is exciting, but it also comes with some uncertainty. However, it has the potential to increase productivity and employee satisfaction. More companies are leveraging technology and adapting their organizational structures and management styles to thrive in this new landscape.

Embracing the work-from-home lifestyle

Working from home can provide enhanced flexibility. However, it's essential to remember that this type of work also requires discipline and balance.

To make the most of your work-from-home experience, finding what works best for you and your unique situation is essential.

Additionally, it's essential to be adaptable and flexible as your needs and circumstances change. Necessary actions may include adjusting your work schedule or discovering innovative ways to maintain motivation and productivity.

If you have the right mindset and approach, working from home, including improved productivity, decreased stress levels, and a work-life balance can benefit you.

Finally, a healthy work-life balance is crucial. You can take breaks and exercise regularly to maintain a healthy and balanced life. It's essential to explore other interests and hobbies and make time for meaningful moments with those close to you. By prioritizing your well-being and happiness, you can avoid stress and fatigue and enjoy the benefits of working from home.

To sum up, succeeding at working from home is not only about the physical space but also about developing a disciplined, adaptable, and resilient mindset. Whether turning every challenge into an opportunity for growth or embracing the flexibility and autonomy of working remotely, those who master the art of working from home can find it a fulfilling and rewarding career choice.

Creating a productive workspace, sticking to a consistent schedule, setting boundaries, communicating effectively, and maintaining a healthy work-life balance are all crucial to harnessing the potential of remote work. However, it's essential to recognize that working from home isn't suitable for everyone and demands discipline, focus, and self-motivation. By practicing and persevering, anyone can learn and improve their ability to work from home effectively.

EPILOGUE

MASTERING THE ART OF WORKING FROM HOME

A new era of work has unfolded in the quiet corners of our homes, where coffee mugs sit beside laptops, and sunlight filters through curtains. The once bustling offices have given way to virtual spaces, and the daily commute has become a stroll from the bedroom to the study. As the dust settles on this transformation, we find ourselves navigating the delicate balance of productivity, well-being, and connection.

1. **Clear Communication Channels

In the digital labyrinth thread. Set up a network of channels —email, instant messaging, video calls—to stay connected with your team. But remember, it's not just about the tools; it's about agreements. Acknowledge different time zones and working hours. Some team members might be juggling family commitments or adjusting to new routines. Clarity fosters collaboration, even across virtual miles.

2. **Stay Focused

Mornings bring promise. Take a breath, sip your coffee, and identify your top three priorities. Break your tasks into manageable chunks. Factor in meetings, but guard against the lure of distractions. The serenity of home can be both a blessing and a curse. Discipline becomes your compass.

3. **Connect, Don't Just Communicate

The camaraderie of the water cooler is now pixels on a screen. Video calls bridge the gap. Look into the camera; let your eyes speak. In the absence of shared office space, intentional small talk becomes essential. Ask about weekends, pets, hobbies—the mundane threads that weave bonds. Remember, rapport thrives on more than just work-related exchanges.

4. **Keep Things Interesting

Virtual meetings need not be monotonous. Unleash the features of your technology canvas. Polls, instant messaging, games—they all have a role. Fact or fiction, anyone? Inject life into the digital ether. Brainstorm, share ideas, and let creativity flow. The screen may separate us, but our imagination knows no bounds.

5. **Set Boundaries and Take Breaks

The Home Office hybrid blurs lines. Define your workspace, both physically and mentally. When the sun dips, shut down the laptop. Step away. Breathe. The world outside awaits. Your well-being fuels your productivity. Remember, breaks are not indulgences; they're necessities.

6. **Check In

Beyond tasks and deadlines, check in on your colleagues. A simple "How are you?" can ripple through the ether, reminding us that we're not isolated souls but interconnected beings. Empathy transcends screens.

7. **Celebrate the Successes

Toast to victories, no matter how small. Have you finished that report? Applaud yourself. Have you navigated a tricky client call? High-five (virtually). Celebrate milestones, for they anchor us on purpose.

8. **Get the Balance Right

The art of working from home lies in equilibrium. The scales tip neither toward burnout nor complacency. It's a dance—a rhythm of work and life, choreographed by you.

And so, as the sun sets on another virtual workday, remember that the canvas of your home holds both challenges and opportunities. Master the strokes, blend the hues, and create a masterpiece where work and life harmonize, and the art of remote work becomes second nature.

May your Wi-Fi signal be strong, your coffee warm, and your heart connected.

AFTERWORD

In the quiet hum of our home offices, where the keyboard clicks blend with the distant sounds of life beyond the screen, we find ourselves immersed in the art of working remotely. The journey from cubicles to kitchen tables has been liberating and challenging—a canvas where we paint our productivity, well-being, and connection.

1. THE SYMPHONY OF SOLITUDE

As the sun sets on another virtual workday, we reflect on the symphony of solitude. The rhythm of our breath replaces the absence of office chatter—the cadence of focus and the crescendo of creativity. We've learned to dance with silence, to find harmony in the quiet. Art is not just about productivity but about the symphony of self-awareness.

2. THE ALCHEMY OF SPACE

Our homes have become alchemical laboratories. We rearrange furniture, chase sunlight, and curate our surroundings. The desk by the window becomes our stage, and the potted plant our muse. We learn that space is more than square footage; it's a vessel for intention—art in transforming corners into sanctuaries, where ideas bloom and resilience thrives.

3. THE TAPESTRY OF CONNECTION

Zoom calls bridge continents, and Slack channels weave threads of camaraderie. We've glimpsed into colleagues' lives —the cat that saunters across the keyboard, the toddler's giggle in the background. The art lies in these glimpses—the humanizing pixels that remind us we're not isolated avatars but interconnected souls.

4. THE PALETTE OF ADAPTABILITY

The commute is now a stroll down the hallway. We've traded suits for pajamas and coffee breaks for kitchen chats. The art lies in adaptability—pivoting from spreadsheets to story time, deadlines to dinner prep. We've become shape-sifters, blending roles seamlessly. The canvas is fluid; the strokes and improvisation.

5. THE COMPASS OF PURPOSE

Beyond tasks and KPIs, we seek purpose. The art lies in aligning keystrokes with meaning. Why do we work? To pay bills, yes—but also to create, connect, and contribute. The distributed workplace invites introspection. We re-calibrate our compass, navigating not just toward goals but toward fulfillment.

6. THE LEGACY OF RESILIENCE

When the world shifted, we adapted. The art lies in resilience—the quiet heroism of showing up, even when the Wi-Fi wavers or the laundry beckons. We've weathered storms, juggled roles, and found strength in vulnerability. The distributed workplace is our legacy—a testament to adaptability, tenacity, and the human spirit.

And so, dear reader, as you close this book, may your workspace be a canvas and your screen a portal to possibility. May you thrive in the distributed workplace, creating art with every keystroke, every pixel, and every heartbeat.

—-

Remember, the art of working remotely is not just about pixels and protocols; it's about the poetry of purpose.*

[1] The concept of remote work has evolved, starting from individuals working from their homes or farms before the Industrial Revolution to the shift towards large factories and offices during the Industrial Revolution.

The invention of the Internet in the 1980s opened up remote work opportunities, revolutionizing how we work and allowing companies and individuals to operate from anywhere, anytime.

The term "telecommuting" was first coined by Jack Nilles, a NASA engineer, and in 1973, IBM conducted a test with a small remote team, showcasing early examples of remote work.

[1]

[1]